TOMATO
TALES

A GARDENER'S JOURNEY FROM SOIL TO SAUCE

[Wietse Jehaes]

Table of Contents

4

INTRODUCTION

Ah, the humble tomato. A fruit disguised as a vegetable, a New World native that's become a cornerstone of Old World cuisines, and a gardening challenge that offers ample rewards—both in taste and pride. Welcome to "Tomato Tales: A Gardener's Journey from Soil to Sauce," where we embark on a voyage through the deep, rich Earth and onto the sun-kissed vines of tomato plants to understand how to grow this versatile crop. And let's not stop there. We'll venture into kitchens and canneries to explore the most delicious ways to preserve and utilize your bounty.

Whether you're a novice looking to start your first vegetable garden or an experienced green thumb seeking to perfect your tomato harvest, this book has something for everyone. The comprehensive chapters are designed to guide you through each phase of the tomato growing process—from selecting the perfect variety for your climate to troubleshooting common issues that can plague even the most meticulous gardener.

The purpose is simple: to offer a definitive, all-in-one guide to mastering the art of tomato cultivation and provide you with many options for using these fruits (yes, fruits!) in many culinary creations.

In Chapter 1, we'll delve into the allure of tomatoes. What makes them so universally loved and grown? We'll discuss their history, nutritional benefits, and place in culture and cuisine. Chapter 2 focuses on soil and location—two overlooked yet critical factors affecting your harvest. This chapter will guide you in preparing your garden for the most optimal tomato growth. The excitement truly begins in Chapter 3, where we discuss sowing the seeds. You'll learn about the importance of seed selection, how to start seeds indoors, and the ins and outs of transplanting your seedlings.

In Chapter 4, we'll move on to nurturing your plants, focusing on essential practices such as watering techniques, mulching, staking, and fertilization. Pests and diseases—every gardener's nightmare—are the focus of Chapter 5. We'll cover organic and chemical methods to keep these nuisances at bay. Finally, the fruits of your labor are ready in Chapter 6, which discusses the harvest. When is the right time to pick your tomatoes? How should you store them? We'll answer these questions and more.

The major focus of Chapter 7 is preserving your crop for future enjoyment. From canning to drying, you'll discover various strategies to guarantee that none of your efforts go to waste. For the more ambitious gardeners, Chapter 8 explores advanced techniques such as pruning, hydroponic systems, and cross-breeding, while Chapter 9 offers inspirational stories from tomato growers worldwide. Chapter 10 will look toward the future, focusing on innovative practices and environmental considerations that every conscientious gardener should know.

Finally, we wrap things up with some parting thoughts and additional resources in Chapter 11. This book is not just a guide on how to grow tomatoes. It's a narrative of the tomato's journey, a celebration of its versatility, and an exploration of the countless joys it brings into our lives— from the garden to the kitchen table and beyond. So let's dig in, shall we? Let's get our hands dirty in the nurturing soil, feel the sun on our faces as we care for our budding plants, and relish the incomparable taste of a homegrown tomato.

Your journey through the world of tomatoes starts now, and I promise, it's a ride you won't want to miss.

CHAPTER-1: THE ALLURE OF TOMATOES
Introduction: Why Tomatoes?

There's a reason the tomato is often the first plant people think of when they imagine a vegetable garden. Or why, for many, summer isn't complete without a juicy tomato slice tucked into a burger or diced over a crisp salad. Tomatoes are the chameleons of the culinary world—equally at home in a rustic sauce, an elegant tart, or even eaten fresh off the vine, still warm from the sun.

Their versatility in the kitchen is unparalleled, but what makes the tomato such an irresistible option for gardeners? But growing tomatoes is an accessible yet rewarding endeavor. With minimal space and effort, you can produce a crop that eclipses store-bought varieties in flavor, nutrition, and overall quality. For many, the homegrown tomato is both a symbol and a measure of gardening prowess—a reflection of the care and love poured into every inch of their garden plot.

The History of Tomato Cultivation

Contrary to popular belief, tomatoes are not native to Italy or any other Mediterranean country. They were first domesticated in South America, and their seeds traveled with explorers and colonists to other parts of the world. Initially met with skepticism in Europe due to their relation to poisonous plants like belladonna, tomatoes were first grown as ornamental curiosities.

It wasn't until the late 17th and early 18th centuries that they began gaining culinary acceptance in Europe. From there, they were incorporated into various recipes and dishes, slowly becoming the kitchen staple we know today. Over the past few centuries, tomato cultivation has seen numerous advances, from the development of hardier, disease-resistant strains to the genetically modified varieties that are the subject of much debate today.

Varieties of Tomatoes

You're spoiled for choice when choosing a type of tomato to grow. From tiny, sweet cherry tomatoes perfect for snacking to large beefsteak varieties that make an entire meal, there's a tomato for every palate and purpose.

Some popular varieties include:

- **Cherry Tomatoes:** Sweet and bite-sized, perfect for salads.
- **Roma Tomatoes:** Elongated with fewer seeds, ideal for sauces and stews.
- **Beefsteak Tomatoes:** Large and juicy, great for slicing.
- **Heirloom Varieties:** Unusual colors, shapes, and flavors. These are often passed down through generations and are a hit among organic gardeners.
- **Hybrids:** Developed for specific growing conditions or resistance to certain diseases.

Each variety has its unique requirements and benefits, which we'll explore in greater detail later on.

Nutritional Benefits of Tomatoes

Beyond their culinary versatility, tomatoes offer a wealth of nutritional benefits. They are high in vitamins A and C, necessary for immunological function and skin health. They are also a good source of fiber and low in calories, making them an excellent choice for anyone watching their weight. Tomatoes are a high source of lycopene, a strong antioxidant that has been examined for its ability to fend against several ailments, including cancer.

The Tomato in Culture and Cuisine

The tomato has inspired artists, chefs, and even filmmakers. It's the star of festivals, the subject of songs, and a beloved character in children's literature. Its role in cuisine is equally varied and influential. From the tomato-rich dishes of Italian cooking to the tangy chutneys of Indian cuisine, tomatoes have a universal appeal that crosses cultural boundaries.

In American culture, the tomato signifies summer, family gatherings, and the joys of home gardening. It is a plant that brings people together, whether sharing gardening tips across a fence or passing a bowl of fresh tomato salad at a picnic.

As we dive deeper into the nuances of growing, harvesting, and cooking with tomatoes, remember that this fruit (technically a fruit!) is more than just a garden staple. It's a piece of history, a nutritional powerhouse, and a symbol of community and culinary versatility. So, let's take this journey from soil to sauce, uncovering the marvelous tomato's wondrous facets.

CHAPTER-2: THE FOUNDATIONS: SOIL AND LOCATION
Types of Soil

Before you even think about planting, it's crucial to understand the soil you're working with. Tomatoes are relatively forgiving, but the right soil can distinguish between a bountiful and disappointing harvest.

Here are the primary types of soil you may encounter:

- **Sandy Soil:** This soil drains well but may lack essential nutrients. It's often too loose to provide good support for tomato plants.
- **Clay Soil:** Rich in nutrients but poor in drainage, clay soil can make it difficult for tomato roots to grow freely. Overwatering can easily lead to root rot.
- **Loamy Soil:** This is the best sort of soil for the majority of gardeners. It's a balanced sand, silt, and

clay mix, offering good drainage and nutrient content.

- **Silt Soil:** Silty soil is fertile but can have poor drainage, much like clay soil.
- **Peaty Soil:** While rich in organic matter, peaty soil is generally too acidic for tomatoes.

Understanding your soil type can help you adjust your planting strategy, whether by amending the soil to improve its nutrient content or selecting tomato varieties better suited to your conditions.

Soil Testing and Preparation

Consider conducting a soil test to understand your soil's condition precisely. Most local agricultural extensions offer this service, or you can purchase DIY soil testing kits. The results will tell you the soil's pH and nutrient levels, vital in determining what amendments are needed.

Tomatoes prefer slightly acidic to neutral soil with a pH range of 6.2 to 6.8. You can adjust your soil with lime or sulfur if it is excessively acidic or alkaline.

Before planting, mixing in organic matter like compost is also advisable. This enriches the soil and improves its texture and drainage—which is essential for growing healthy tomatoes.

Choosing the Right Location

Tomatoes adore the sun and need at least 6 to 8 hours of direct sunlight daily. Lack of adequate sunlight can lead to poor fruit development and make the plants more susceptible to disease.

Your selected location should also have good drainage. Prolonged periods of waterlogged soil can lead to root rot and other diseases. If your only available space is prone to poor drainage, consider raised beds or container gardening as alternatives.

Climate Considerations

While tomatoes prefer warm conditions, they are sensitive to extremes. Intense heat can cause blossom drop, while frost can kill the plants outright. This is why understanding your local climate and growing season is so important.

In colder locations, you may wish to start early by growing seeds inside or choosing early harvest cultivars. In hotter climates, choose heat-tolerant varieties and consider providing some afternoon shade to protect the plants from extreme temperatures.

Container vs. Ground Planting

Tomatoes can thrive both in the ground and containers, but each has its benefits and limitations:

- **Ground Planting:** Allows for larger plants and potentially higher yields. However, it requires more prep work, such as soil testing and possible amendments.
- **Container Planting:** Ideal for those with limited space or poor soil. Containers offer better drainage and are easier to move, allowing you to take advantage of the best sunlight or bring the plants indoors in adverse weather.

Remember, the container should be at least 18 inches in diameter to give the roots ample room to grow and have good drainage holes.

With the right soil and the perfect location, you're setting the stage for a tomato crop that could be the envy of the neighborhood. The next step is to sow your seeds, and we'll move to Chapter 3: Sowing the Seeds. But as you proceed, remember that, like building a home, the foundation is key. Good soil and an ideal location are the cornerstones upon which your tomato empire will rise.

CHAPTER-3: SOWING THE SEEDS
Seed Selection

Your journey from soil to sauce begins with a seed, but not just any seed will do. The type of tomato you want to grow will depend on your culinary needs, available space, and local climate. Here's a quick guide to help you decide:

- **Determinate Varieties:** These plants grow to a fixed height and produce all their fruit simultaneously, which is excellent for canning or making sauce. Examples include 'Roma' and 'Bush Early Girl.'
- **Indeterminate Varieties:** These produce fruit throughout the growing season, offering a prolonged harvest. Examples include 'Cherry' and 'Beefsteak.'
- **Early Season Varieties:** These are suitable for areas with short growing seasons as they mature quickly.
- **Heirlooms** are traditional varieties that have not been hybridized, often prized for their unique flavors and colors.

- **Hybrids:** These are bred for specific characteristics like disease resistance or uniform size.

Starting Seeds Indoors

For many gardeners, starting seeds indoors gives the plants a head start, especially in regions with shorter growing seasons. Here's how to go about it:

1. **Timing:** Start 6-8 weeks before your area's last expected frost date.
2. **Containers:** Use seed trays or small pots with drainage holes.
3. **Soil:** Opt for a light, seed-starting mix for good drainage.
4. **Planting:** Plant seeds about 1/4-inch deep.
5. **Temperature:** Keep the soil warm, between 70-80°F, to encourage germination.
6. **Light:** Once the seedlings emerge, place them under fluorescent lights or near a south-facing window where they can get plenty of light.

Transplanting Seedlings

After the danger of frost has passed and your seedlings have at least two sets of true leaves, it's time to transplant them into their final growing location. Here's how:

1. **Hardening Off:** Gradually acclimate the seedlings to outdoor conditions over 7-10 days.
2. **Spacing:** Indeterminate varieties need more space (about 24–36 inches apart) than determinate types (18–24 inches apart).
3. **Planting Depth:** Plant them deep so that two-thirds of the plant is underground to encourage strong root development.

Outdoor Sowing

Direct sowing is viable if you live in a region with a long growing season. Wait until all frost crisis has passed and the soil has warmed up. Then:

1. **Prepare the Soil:** Improve the soil and incorporate some compost.

2. **Planting Depth:** Plant seeds about 1/4-inch deep.

3. **Spacing:** As with transplanted seedlings, respect the space requirements for your chosen variety.

The Importance of Spacing

Proper spacing is more than just an aesthetic choice. It can impact air circulation, sunlight penetration, and even the prevalence of diseases. Overcrowded plants are less productive and more susceptible to mold and fungal infections. Always refer to the specific recommendations for the tomato variety you're growing, and when in doubt, err on the side of giving the plants more room to grow.

Whether you're starting from seed or transplanting a seedling, the initial steps you take will greatly influence the health and yield of your tomato plants. In the next chapter, we'll delve into the care and keeping of your burgeoning tomato garden—from watering and fertilizing to staking and beyond. Because while it's true that all good things start from a seed, they also require a gardener's guiding hand to reach their full potential.

CHAPTER-4: NURTURING THE GROWTH
Watering Techniques

Water is life, especially for tomatoes, but how much is enough? Too little and the plants may not fruit well; too much and you risk diseases like root rot. Here's the lowdown on watering:

- **Consistency is Key:** Aim for a consistent watering schedule. Inconsistent watering can lead to problems like blossom end rot and fruit cracking.
- **Early Morning Watering:** It's best to water your plants early in the morning to minimize evaporation loss and give them enough moisture to get through the day.
- **Soaker Hoses and Drip Systems:** These can deliver water directly to the root zone, minimizing wastage and reducing foliage wetness that could lead to diseases.

Mulching and Weed Control

Mulch is a gardener's best friend. It serves several purposes:

- **Weed Control:** Mulch suppresses weeds that compete with your tomatoes for nutrients.
- **Moisture Retention:** A good layer of mulch can help retain moisture, reducing the need for frequent watering.
- **Temperature Control:** Mulch functions as an insulator, cooling the soil in the summer and warming it in the spring and fall.

Organic mulches like straw or shredded leaves are excellent choices. Avoid using grass clippings unless you're sure they're free of herbicides.

Staking and Support

Tomato plants, particularly indeterminate varieties, need support to keep them off the ground, where they're more susceptible to pests and diseases. Here are some popular methods:

- **Cages:** Tomato cages offer good support and are easy to install but can be cumbersome in small spaces.
- **Stakes:** Wooden or metal stakes can be used for individual plants and offer excellent support. Use soft ties to secure branches to the stakes.
- **Trellising:** This involves creating a horizontal support structure for plants. It's more labor-intensive but excellent for small spaces and large-scale gardens.

Fertilization

Tomatoes are heavy feeders, requiring good nutrients, especially nitrogen, phosphorus, and potassium.

- **Timing:** Fertilize when you first transplant and again when the fruits are about the size of a golf ball.
- **Type:** Use a balanced fertilizer or one specially formulated for tomatoes. Avoid high-nitrogen fertilizers as they promote leaf growth over fruiting.

Signs of Healthy Growth

How do you know if all your efforts are paying off? Here are some signs:

- **Vibrant Green Leaves:** Yellow or brown leaves could indicate nutrient deficiencies or diseases.
- **Strong Stems:** Weak stems can't support the fruit and are a sign of inadequate light or nutrients.
- **Flower Formation:** Lack of flowers means no fruit. This could be due to too much nitrogen or inadequate light.
- **Healthy Root System:** While not always visible, a healthy root system is essential for nutrient uptake.

Growing tomatoes is a journey filled with lessons in patience, attentiveness, and care. Every stake you place, every drop of water you provide, and every leaf you inspect brings you closer to a fruitful harvest. The following chapter will review the problems and remedies associated with pests and illnesses because even the most seasoned gardeners experience setbacks. But armed with the knowledge from this chapter, you're well-equipped to nurture your tomato plants to their full potential.

CHAPTER-5: PEST AND DISEASE MANAGEMENT

Common Tomato Pests

Growing tomatoes is not without its challenges. The tender leaves and juicy fruit are a veritable smorgasbord for garden pests. Let's take a look at some of the most common offenders.

1. **Tomato Hornworms**: These green caterpillars with a "horn" are voracious eaters that can defoliate a plant almost overnight.

2. **Aphids**: Tiny, soft-bodied insects that feed on the sap of your tomato plants, often found on the underside of leaves. They're notorious for transmitting diseases.

3. **Whiteflies**: Similar to aphids but white, they suck the sap and weaken the plant.

4. **Cutworms**: These soil-dwelling pests cut young plants at their base.

5. **Spider Mites**: Tiny spider-like pests that suck plant juices, causing stippling on leaves.
6. **Leaf Miners**: The larvae of these insects tunnel through the leaves, leaving behind winding trails.
7. **Stink Bugs**: These bugs feed on fruits, causing distortions and affecting ripening.

Understanding your enemy is the first step to creating a defense. Research each pest's lifecycle to identify vulnerable stages when control measures would be most effective.

Common Diseases

Pests aren't the only problems; various diseases can spell disaster for your tomato crop.

1. **Early Blight**: Identified by dark spots on older leaves, this fungal disease can decimate your plants if not controlled.
2. **Late Blight**: Unlike early blight, this affects the leaves, stem, and fruit and can wipe out your entire crop in damp weather.

3. **Fusarium Wilt**: A soil-borne disease that causes yellowing and wilting, starting from the lower leaves.
4. **Verticillium Wilt**: Similar to Fusarium wilt, but generally affects plants later in the season.
5. **Blossom End Rot**: Caused by calcium deficiency, resulting in dark, sunken spots at the fruit's blossom end.
6. **Tomato Mosaic Virus**: Stunts growth and causes mosaic patterns on leaves.
7. **Root Knot Nematodes**: These microscopic worms cause lumps or 'knots' in roots, leading to stunted growth and reduced yield.

Organic Control Methods

Being conscious of the environment while keeping pests and diseases at bay is no small feat. Here are some organic options:

1. **Insecticidal Soap**: Effective for soft-bodied insects like aphids and whiteflies.
2. **Neem Oil**: It kills pests and prevents numerous illnesses by acting as an insecticide and fungicide.

3. **Beneficial Insects**: Introduce predators like ladybugs to control aphids.
4. **Crop Rotation**: Shifting the plants planted in certain plots aids in the prevention of soil-borne illnesses.
5. **Compost Tea** is a foliar spray that can help prevent fungal diseases.
6. **Garlic or Pepper Spray**: Homemade sprays can repel various pests.

Chemical Control Options

Sometimes, the situation may call for chemical solutions, but following guidelines and recommendations is crucial.

1. **Pyrethroids**: These synthetic insecticides are effective but can harm beneficial insects.
2. **Fungicides**: Products containing copper or sulfur can be effective against blight.
3. **Systemic Insecticides**: Absorbed by the plant, these provide longer-lasting protection but may have environmental impacts.

Always read the label, wear protective gear, and observe the waiting period before harvest.

Prevention Strategies

Prevention is always better than cure.

1. **Regular Monitoring**: Watch for the earliest signs of pests and diseases to act swiftly.

2. **Healthy Soil**: A balanced, nutrient-rich soil generally produces robust plants that are naturally more resistant to pests and diseases.

3. **Proper Spacing**: Well-spaced plants ensure good air circulation, reducing humidity and the likelihood of fungal diseases.

4. **Cleanliness**: Keep the garden free from plant debris, which can serve as a breeding ground for pests and diseases.

5. **Quarantine**: New plants should be kept separate until you're sure they're disease-free.

In conclusion, growing tomatoes requires a vigilant eye and proactive management to effectively deal with pests and diseases. Whether you prefer organic methods, chemical controls, or a combination, keeping these uninvited guests in check is critical for a bountiful harvest. By following these tips and strategies, you can look forward to the joys of plucking ripe, juicy tomatoes from your very own garden.

CHAPTER-6: THE HARVEST

The journey from seed to sauce is an intricate tapestry of care, anticipation, and patience. After tending your tomato plants through sprouting, growing, and flowering, the pinnacle of your gardening journey is the harvest.

When to Harvest

Determining the right time to harvest your tomatoes involves more than eyeing the reddest fruit on the vine. Factors to consider include:

1. **Color**: When ripe, most tomatoes turn from green to deep red, pink, or yellow. However, color can be misleading; some heirloom varieties remain green when ripe.

2. **Texture**: Ripe tomatoes have a uniform firmness. If the fruit is hard near the stem but softer at the bottom, it may need more time.

3. **Aroma**: Tomatoes give off a strong, sweet aroma when fully ripe. Sniff around the stem end for this signature smell.

4. **Ease of Release**: When twisted gently, a ripe tomato should easily detach from the vine. If you have to exert force, it's likely not yet ready.

5. **Days to Maturity**: Check the seed packet for information on how many days it typically takes for the variety to ripen.

Methods of Harvesting

Once you've determined that it's time to pick your tomatoes, you'll want to follow best practices for harvesting to ensure the fruit remains in pristine condition.

1. **Hand-Picking**: This is the most common method. Gently twist and pull the fruit or use pruning shears to snip it off, leaving a short piece of stem attached.

2. **Tray Harvesting**: For small, cherry-type tomatoes, you can use a shallow tray to catch fruit as you snip the clusters from the vine.

3. **Whole-Vine Harvest**: In frost-prone locations, pick the entire plant and hang it upside-down in a garage or basement to allow the remaining tomatoes to ripen.

Post-Harvest Care

Once your tomatoes are picked, the work isn't quite done. Proper care can extend their shelf-life and improve flavor.

1. **Cleaning**: A gentle rinse to remove dirt and lingering insects is usually sufficient.
2. **Curing**: Though not common for tomatoes, some gardeners swear by letting freshly picked tomatoes sit in a sunny, warm location for 2-3 days to improve flavor.
3. **Sorting**: Separate your tomatoes by ripeness and any signs of disease or pest damage to prevent spoilage.

Storing Tomatoes

Storage can make or break your hard-won harvest. Consider the following:

1. **Room Temperature**: Tomatoes continue to ripen at room temperature and are best stored stem side down on a flat surface.

2. **Refrigeration**: While it can prolong shelf-life, refrigeration can lead to mealy, flavorless tomatoes. Use this option only for overly ripe tomatoes you can't consume quickly.

3. **Freezing**: For long-term storage, consider freezing whole tomatoes or processed forms like sauce or paste.

Troubleshooting Common Harvest Issues

Even with the best care, you may encounter issues during the harvest.

1. **Cracking**: Rapid changes in temperature and moisture levels can lead to cracked fruit. Consistent watering can help mitigate this.

2. **Blossom End Rot**: As discussed in the previous chapter, this is caused by calcium deficiency and needs to be addressed during the growing phase.

3. **Uneven Ripening**: Caused by nutrient imbalances, pests, or diseases, uneven ripening can ruin the aesthetics and flavor of your tomatoes. Timely intervention is essential.

Harvesting is not merely plucking fruit from a vine but celebrating months of hard work, vigilance, and a little bit of luck from Mother Nature. As you savor the fruits of your labor—whether in a salad, as a sauce or straight off the vine—each bite becomes a story, a culmination of your Tomato Tale.

CHAPTER-7: PRESERVING THE BOUNTY

So you've harvested your tomatoes. Whether it's a modest haul from a couple of plants or an overwhelming abundance from a dedicated tomato garden, the next question arises: What to do with all these tomatoes? The answer lies in the art of preservation.

Canning Tomatoes

One of the most popular methods for long-term storage of tomatoes is canning. The process involves several steps:

1. **Preparation**: Wash your tomatoes thoroughly. Remove any stems and leaves.
2. **Blanching**: Boil the tomatoes for 30-60 seconds, then plunge them into icy water. This will loosen the skin and make removal easier.
3. **Skinning and Seeding**: Peel off the tomato skins and remove the seeds if desired.

4. **Sterilization**: Sterilize your canning jars and lids by boiling them for 10 minutes.

5. **Filling**: Pack the tomatoes tightly into the jars, leaving about half an inch of space at the top.

6. **Boiling**: Seal the jars and boil them for a specified time (usually 35-45 minutes for quarts).

7. **Cooling and Storing**: Once boiled, let the jars cool to room temperature, ensuring the lids have sealed correctly. Store in a cool, dark place.

Making Tomato Sauce and Paste

Tomato sauce and paste are excellent options for those interested in prepping ingredients for future meals.

Tomato Sauce

1. **Cooking**: Combine skinned and seeded tomatoes in a pot. Add spices like basil, oregano, garlic, and salt to taste.

2. **Simmering**: Cook the mixture on low heat until it thickens.

3. **Blending**: Use a blender or a food processor to achieve a smooth consistency.
4. **Canning or Freezing**: You can scan the sauce, like whole tomatoes, or freeze it in airtight containers.

Tomato Paste

1. **Reducing**: Cook tomato sauce over low heat until it becomes extremely thick.
2. **Straining**: Some people strain the reduced sauce through a fine mesh for a smoother consistency.
3. **Storing**: Freeze the paste in ice cube trays for easy portioning or canned for long-term storage.

Freezing Methods

Frozen tomatoes are a quick and easy way to preserve them.

1. **Whole Tomatoes**: Wash and dry whole tomatoes, place them on a baking sheet to freeze individually, and then transfer to a Ziploc bag.
2. **Chopped Tomatoes**: Before putting tomatoes in bags, dice or slice them and freeze them on a baking sheet.

3. **Tomato Sauce or Paste**: Freeze in airtight containers or ice cube trays.

Drying and Dehydrating

Dehydrated tomatoes are flavorful and can be used in a variety of dishes.

1. **Oven-Drying**: Slice tomatoes thinly and place them on a baking sheet. Dry in the oven at a low temperature (around 200°F) for 6-12 hours.
2. **Dehydrator**: You can achieve more consistent results if you have a dehydrator. Follow your machine's guidelines for tomatoes.
3. **Storing**: Store in an airtight container, preferably in a cool, dark place. Some people also store dried tomatoes in olive oil.

Creative Tomato Recipes

Your bounty can be more than just preserved; it can be transformed.

1. **Tomato Chutney**: This can be a tangy accompaniment to many dishes.

2. **Sun-Dried Tomato Pesto**: Use your oven-dried tomatoes to whip up a tasty pesto.

3. **Tomato Soup**: Make a large batch and freeze portions for comforting meals throughout winter.

4. **Stuffed Tomatoes**: These can be filled with a grain and vegetable mix and then frozen for later.

5. **Tomato Jam**: A sweet and savory tomato jam pairs excellently with meats and cheeses.

Preserving your tomatoes is about more than just prolonging their shelf-life; it's about capturing the essence of summer in a jar, bag, or bottle. Each preservation method offers extended storage and unique flavors and uses, further enhancing tomatoes' role in your meals. This chapter ensures that your Tomato Tales can continue long after the growing season has ended.

CHAPTER-8: BEYOND THE BASICS: ADVANCED TECHNIQUES

After mastering the fundamental practices of growing tomatoes, you may be interested in pushing the boundaries of what you can achieve. The world of tomato cultivation is vast, and many techniques and approaches can help you optimize yield, flavor, and even the size of your tomatoes. Welcome to the advanced course in tomato growing.

Pruning and Training

Pruning isn't just for rose bushes; your tomato plants can also benefit significantly.

1. **Selective Pruning**: Remove the lower leaves and branches that touch the ground to improve airflow and minimize disease.

2. **Suckers**: These shoots grow in the axils between the leaves and the stem. Some growers remove these to direct more energy into fruit production.

3. **Staking and Trellising**: Pruning goes hand in hand with training your plants to grow on stakes or trellises. This method allows for better light penetration and easier harvesting.

4. **Top Pruning**: Cutting off the top part of the plant late in the season can direct energy into ripening existing fruits rather than producing new ones.

Hydroponic and Aquaponic Systems

Soilless growing systems have their own sets of benefits and challenges.

1. **Hydroponics**: This involves growing plants in nutrient-rich water. It allows for precise control of nutrients and faster growth but requires specialized equipment.

2. **Aquaponics**: This combines aquaculture (raising fish) and hydroponics. The fish waste provides an organic nutrient source for the plants, and the plants help filter and purify the water.

3. **System Types**: From Deep Water Culture to Nutrient Film Technique, various systems can be employed depending on your space and needs.

Cross-breeding and Hybridization

1. **Pollination**: Learning to pollinate flowers manually can enable you to cross different tomato varieties.

2. **Seed Collection**: Harvest and store seeds from your best tomatoes for future planting.

3. **Natural Variants**: Over time, you might discover a plant that shows unique and desirable traits. By selectively breeding this plant, you can develop your tomato variety.

Heirlooms vs. Hybrids

1. **Heirlooms**: These are open-pollinated varieties that have been passed down through generations. They are often more flavorful but may be less disease-resistant.
2. **Hybrids**: These result from controlled cross-pollination between two different parent plants. They often have enhanced disease resistance and more consistent yields but can be less flavorful.
3. **Experiment**: Try growing both types to determine which qualities—flavor, yield, disease resistance—you prioritize.

Growing Giant Tomatoes

Perhaps you're interested in more than just a tasty harvest; maybe you're aiming for record-breaking fruit.

1. **Varietal Selection**: Start with a known "giant" variety like 'Belmonte' or 'Delicious.'
2. **Pruning**: Focus the plant's energy on a single fruit by removing competing fruits and possibly even leaves.

3. **Nutrition**: Specialized fertilizers and growth hormones can sometimes maximize size, although these can sacrifice flavor.
4. **Support**: Make sure the infrastructure is in place to support a massive tomato; specialized slings or nets can help.

This chapter explores advanced techniques and ideas to help you take your tomato growing to the next level. Whether you want to delve into hydroponics, create your tomato variety, or even grow a giant tomato, there's always something more to learn in the ever-expanding world of tomato cultivation. Your Tomato Tales are limited only by your imagination and your willingness to experiment.

CHAPTER-9: TOMATO TALES: STORIES FROM GARDENERS

After navigating the vast world of tomato cultivation—from the basics to the advanced techniques—you might wonder how these theories and methods play out in real-world scenarios. This chapter brings diverse stories from gardeners who have walked various paths in their tomato-growing journeys. These narratives can offer you insights, inspiration, and perhaps even a sense of community.

Backyard Tomato Gardeners

Sarah from Michigan

Sarah started with a small garden bed in her suburban backyard. Over the years, she's experimented with heirloom varieties and found her family's favorite: 'Brandywine Pink.' Sarah highlights the importance of soil testing. "Each winter, I get my soil tested, and it's like a report card for my garden," she says.

Carlos from California

A tech worker by day, Carlos uses IoT (Internet of Things) sensors to monitor soil moisture and automate watering. His 'San Marzano' tomatoes are the talk of the neighborhood. "Technology can be a great ally in the garden. It's not cheating; it's optimizing," Carlos believes.

Commercial Tomato Farming

Green Valley Farms

Located in the heartland of Ohio, this commercial farm focuses on 'Roma' tomatoes grown hydroponically. The farm prioritizes sustainability, using solar energy to power its operations. "People think big farms don't care about the environment. We want to prove them wrong," says owner Margaret.

Organic Vines Co.

This organic farm in Oregon swears by companion planting, using basil and marigolds to deter pests from their tomato crops naturally. They primarily grow 'Cherokee Purple' tomatoes and distribute them to local farmer's markets.

Urban Tomato Gardens

Brooklyn Roof Garden

Anna transformed her Brooklyn apartment's roof into a tomato haven using containers. She grows smaller varieties like 'Tiny Tim' and 'Tumbling Tom.' "Space shouldn't limit your gardening dreams," Anna emphasizes.

Community Garden in Chicago

An inner-city community garden in Chicago offers plots for residents to grow vegetables, including various tomatoes. The garden has become a hub for community interaction and education. "It's not just about the tomatoes; it's about the people," says community leader Jamal.

Community Gardens and Co-ops

The Green Share Co-op

Located in Vermont, this co-op allows members to share tools, seeds, and, most importantly, knowledge. Seasonal tomato-tasting events are a community favorite.

Atlanta Educational Garden

This community garden focuses on educating children about gardening. Tomatoes are a big hit because they're easy to grow and provide quick gratification. "The kids love seeing the fruits of their labor," says educator Emily.

Exotic Locations and Unique Challenges

Arctic Tomato Tales

Sophia, a researcher in Alaska, uses a geothermal greenhouse to grow tomatoes. The extreme conditions make it challenging, but Sophia says, "If tomatoes can grow here, they can grow anywhere."

Tomatoes on a Boat

John, a retired sailor, cultivates tomatoes on his houseboat. He enjoys fresh tomatoes while cruising along the coast using a hydroponic system. "Your garden travels with you," John chuckles.

These stories highlight the infinite pathways in the world of tomato growing. Each tale is a testament to this humble fruit's versatility, resilience, and community-building power. As you venture further into your Tomato Tales, remember that every challenge and triumph adds another layer to your personal story in the vast anthology of tomato cultivation.

CHAPTER-10: CONCLUSIONS AND FUTURE PROSPECTS

Reflecting on the Journey

As we reach the end of this book, let's pause for a moment to reflect on the incredible journey we've undertaken. From understanding the historical significance of tomatoes and the variety of types to discussing the best practices in soil preparation, seed sowing, nurturing growth, and harvest, we have delved deep into the art and science of tomato cultivation.

Our journey has been inclusive, covering the entire gamut of tomato growing from the hobbyist's backyard to commercial farms. We've even ventured into tales of tomatoes in exotic locations, hydroponic systems, and community gardens' bustling environment.

We have done more than learn how to grow tomatoes; we've enriched our understanding of what it means to cultivate a living thing, to be custodians of nature, and to derive both sustenance and pleasure from a simple fruit that has become an integral part of global cuisines. Whether you are a seasoned gardener or a novice, there's always something new to learn and explore in the ever-evolving world of tomatoes.

Innovations in Tomato Growing

The field of tomato cultivation is not static. It's dynamic and ever-evolving, thanks to the efforts of scientists, researchers, and passionate gardeners. Innovations are happening quickly, from developing disease-resistant varieties to tomatoes that can be grown in extreme conditions, like high salinity soils or drought-prone areas.

Modern technologies such as drones and sensors are also making their way into commercial tomato farms to monitor plant health and soil conditions and predict the best harvest times. Artificial intelligence and machine learning algorithms are being created to detect pests and illnesses in their early stages.

The Internet of Things (IoT) is another frontier in tomato farming. Smart irrigation systems can be controlled remotely, ensuring the optimal water use. Greenhouses can be automated to adjust temperature, humidity, and light conditions according to the needs of the tomato plants.

These advancements make tomato cultivation more efficient and sustainable, which is crucial for the planet and future generations.

Environmental Concerns

As we look toward the future, we can't ignore the environmental impact of agriculture, including tomato cultivation. Traditional farming methods have often relied on the heavy use of fertilizers and pesticides, contributing to soil degradation, water pollution, and harm to beneficial insects and animals.

But the tide is turning. Organic farming, sustainable approaches, and integrated pest management are becoming increasingly popular. Many gardeners are choosing to grow heirloom varieties, which, aside from their unique flavors and textures, are often better adapted to local conditions and require fewer inputs.

Additionally, initiatives are underway to reduce the carbon footprint of tomato cultivation by employing renewable energy sources and reducing waste in the supply chain. Water recycling and rainwater harvesting are becoming more common in small and large operations.

The Future of Tomato Cultivation

As we move forward, it's clear that a blend of tradition and innovation will shape the future of tomato cultivation. While we'll continue to value and preserve age-old practices and heirloom varieties, we'll also adopt cutting-edge technologies and methods for efficiency and sustainability.

Community-driven efforts are expected to play a significant role, as well. Sharing knowledge, seeds, and resources within community gardens and online platforms can empower more people to grow tomatoes, promoting food security and biodiversity.

Moreover, there is an increasing awareness of the social and therapeutic benefits of gardening. Growing tomatoes is not just about the end product but also the process. Nurturing a plant from seed to fruit can offer immense personal satisfaction and a sense of accomplishment.

Final Thoughts

Tomatoes are more than just a staple food item; they symbolize life's incredible diversity and richness. From the tiny, sweet cherry tomato to the hefty, robust beefsteak, each variety has its own story and unique journey from soil to sauce.

As you close this book, I hope you feel enlightened and inspired. May your hands get dirty with soil, your garden teems with life, and your kitchen be filled with the luscious aroma of tomatoes in every form—from freshly sliced to simmering sauce.

The future of tomatoes is as bright as their vibrant hues, and you, the gardener, are a pivotal part of that future. Keep growing, learning, and, most importantly, savoring the joy and richness that tomatoes bring our lives.

Here's to many more seasons of abundant harvests and delicious tomato dishes. Thank you for being a part of this journey.

And so, dear reader, this concludes our voyage through the world of tomatoes. But as any gardener will tell you, the end of one season is just the beginning of another. Here's to new beginnings and the evergreen allure of the tomato.

CONCLUSION

As we close the final pages of this book, it's important to understand that the journey with tomatoes doesn't end here. It's a lifelong adventure filled with surprises, challenges, and, most importantly, growth. While this book aims to be comprehensive, covering all the aspects you need to know about growing tomatoes successfully, it is just a starting point, a cornerstone to build your tomato-growing endeavors. You'll discover that as you go along, you will accumulate a lot of practical wisdom that goes beyond the written word. Every season will be a new lesson. Sometimes, you'll face new challenges—unexpected pests, new diseases, or climate anomalies. Other times, you'll relish the pure delight of a bumper harvest or the discovery of a new heirloom variety that thrives in your soil.

We all stand on the shoulders of the farmers, gardeners, and scientists who have come before us. The knowledge surrounding tomato cultivation has been passed down through generations, enriched by modern innovations. It's a heritage of shared wisdom. So, as you become more proficient in growing tomatoes, consider sharing your experiences and insights through social media, local community gardens, or even writing your guide. Knowledge grows when it is shared. There is an expansive and supportive community of tomato enthusiasts, both online and offline. Forums, blogs, social media groups, and community gardens allow you to connect, share, and learn. You'll find that even the most seasoned tomato growers are often keen to exchange tips, troubleshoot problems, and celebrate successes. Engaging with this community can offer additional learning and enjoyment to your tomato-growing journey.

As stewards of the Earth, we are responsible for practicing and promoting sustainable gardening. From opting for organic methods to conserving water and promoting local biodiversity, every little effort counts. As you progress in your journey, you'll find that sustainability and gardening go hand in hand, each enriching the other in a virtuous cycle. If there's one thing to take away from this book, let it be this: growing tomatoes is not just an agricultural act; it's an act of connection. Connection with the soil, nature, history, and community. Each tomato you grow is a testament to this interconnectedness, a small but significant tribute to the intricate web of life.

So, go ahead, sow those seeds, nurture those plants, harvest those fruits, and savor the flavorful bounty. Here's to your tomato tales, from soil to sauce, and the many adventures await. Thank you for joining me on this educational and inspiring journey through "Tomato Tales: A Gardener's Journey from Soil to Sauce." May your gardens be ever fruitful and your hearts be ever full. Happy Gardening!

<-END->

Printed in Great Britain
by Amazon